The Astronomy Of Love

AF211365

I'm coming
From the stars
Piece by piece
One layer at a time
Eventually
I'm ready
As a person
To humanity
To equality
To you
To love
I'm shining my own light
If you see me
When you look at the sky
Come to me
And we form
Our own galaxy.

Everything Is Near Me

I looked long too far
I didn't see the details
I dreamed something
Somewhere
I was inside my story book
I believed
In the images of the mind
However
The reality was
Close to me
Under my eyes
I was a long time blind
But now I can see
You
There
Near
Where you have been
All the time
My whole life.

Empathy Is The Responsibility

I live
That's enough for me
But
If I live alone
That's not enough
For anyone else
Alone you don't see
The others
Alone you don't know
The others
Alone you don't understand
Empathy
No responsibility
For any other ones
Empathy
Is the responsibility.

Dialog

I am the one
You're the something else
Infinite and different
I see in you
And I see otherwise

The world is here
Thou art more
I need your touch
Create my world.

© 2017 Kolamo, Mika
Kustantaja: BoD – Books on Demand,
Helsinki, Suomi
Valmistaja: BoD – Books on Demand,
Norderstedt, Saksa
ISBN: 978-951-568-284-0

Equation

When I am
Equally
I am
Alone

When I am many
I am
The one.

Blessed Fist

I'm kneeling deep
Father
Son
Holy Spirit

In my fist
Lives the truth
I'm a servant of the truth

I'm lost
The truth of mine
Is just a servant's truth.

I Enjoy The Silence

I've been living a long time
Many bends
Many upphills
I have learned
Piece by piece
My life

Today I understand
I'm not in a hurry
To anything
Time is always there
I enjoy
The silence
Inside me.

The Fatal Coincidence

I sat on the bed
I was alone
I looked at the pictures
I was silent
Than dead
Suddenly
You were in it
Than emptiness
Would have been fulfilled
In one nanosecond
I felt
Like I was alive
By chance
Protected by destiny.

The Feeling Of Freedom

Clock in hand
I'm breathing
I look forward to tomorrow
I close my eyes
I'm scared

When the door opens
I walk out
When I walk
I finally understand

Eureka!

Fix Me, I'll Fix You

I have bugs in me
I'm not perfect
I don't know everything
I want to learn myself
Fix me
Then
At the same time
I'll fix you
Together
We are perfect.

The Flower Who Smiled For Me

I walked
I was watching
Meadows and fields
I was looking for
The special flower
For a long time
Patiently
Finally
Hard work
Brought the prize
I found the flower
Who smiled
For me
The most beautiful moment
Of my life
Was
In that smile.

I Found You From The Sky

I looked at the sky
Without a telescope
I looked closely
Calmly
Without hurry
Eventually
I saw one star there
It was burning
Far more than others
Among millions of stars
I saw only one star
You.

The Importance Of A Moment

When I see
My experience accumulates
When I feel
My views accumulate
For a moment
The moment is here and now
Tomorrow
Was yesterday.

Intersection

The clock is ticking
The mind is filled
The path turns into a road
The road turns into the constellation
The constellation becomes chaos

I go back to the start
A different intersection
The same direction.

The Journey

I look at my own mirror
My reflection is walking all the time
He is afraid to stop
He is walking fast

Even though he would walk
How long anyway
How fast anyway
He would carry his own place
Somewhere
Where he would be the same he.

The Light And The Darkness

In the light
I see a lot
The details
They form a whole

In the darkness
I see inside me
The details
They form a whole

No light is needed
For thinking
Thinking is always
There.

Love Is A Storm In The Blood

Mistakes
Wrong words
Bad air
Broken
Life

Nothing is enough
If you are not valid
Still
Love doesn't stop
It's a storm in the blood
In molecules' ocean.

Love Is My Religion

I felt your body
After
I learned your mind
I felt your mind
After
I learned your body
Your body is my temple
Where I worship
Your mind
Which is my guide
To understand myself
Love is my religion.

The Minute Of My Life

I look through the window
The universe is out
One minute and I die
I leave a mark from my life
To the window

The relative...
If I can't see myself
There is no time
No any minutes.

Monuments And Statues

Rocky glances in granite
Feelings are carved in stone
Ideas in time
I will plunge inside to me
And I feel it again
I'm like you all others

I'm a monument from a man
I stand as a statue through my life.

On My Street

I'm talking a lot
With bold words
With all my heart
Time is running
It's the law of life
I do not care
From the thoughts of others
If I can walk freely
On my street

I'm on the way
With bold steps
As a whole individual
Time is running
It's a universal law
I do not care
From the talks of others
If I can walk freely
On my street.

On The Line

Life is a line
Curve and straight
Sometimes short
Shorten to the end

Line has points
The infinite amount
Within a limited time
Everyone is in order
But I'm moving
Either now
Or tomorrow.

Output

I

Open the front door
No keyholes
Of which peep

I breathe
Clean air.

My Own Star Is Visible In The Light Of The Stars

I looked into dark heaven
For a long time
Far away shines
A star
Several stars
I knew the physics
Starry sky
Patterns
Facts of the orbits
It was enough for me today
That
I was in the light
And I stood there
Next to you
Just you
You are the star.

Pair Of Equations

I was surprised
I had been alone for a long time
I was used to
Into myself
I had solved every day
The equations of my life
Little different ones
But always
Same parameters
Familiar formulas

Then
You came from
You mixed my calculations
My clear mind formulas
I didn't know anymore
Than one equation
Two equations are created
From two variables
And solving it
It's needed
Both.

Physicist's Mental Landscape

I love symmetry
Endless possibilities
Snowflakes
Diamonds
Reflections

Symmetry is more
Endless impossibilities
Which is not true
What can't happen
And when some would think of it

Then I am certain
Everything that happens

What can happen
Finally also occurs.

Reconciliation

Too long
I lived for myself
Too long
Nobody else
Was nothing
It was just me
I saw only myself
Every moment
Even then
I wasn't there
Where I was always
As an egoist
As a narcissist

Time has come
To turn time counterclockwise
Now I can see a little
But still very little
The journey is long
Over the Himalayas
In my mind
And many times again
Reconciliation
Is just in the beginning.

The Rising

I was lost
For a long time
Too long
I didn't feel myself
I didn't know myself
I wasn't strong
I wasn't enough
Not even for myself
I didn't trust myself
Nothing in me

Now
I have solved the problem
The most difficult equation
Of my mind
Myself here
In my life
With others
And their lives
I enjoy it a bit
Piece at a time
I won't live
I live.

River

Flowing
Seething
Rapids and bays
Changing its shape
But the water doesn't stop
Never
Let's love.

The Road Is Light For A Little While

I walked long in the dark
Thanks for that
If I didn't walk
I wouldn't see
The most important things
The best things of my life
Understanding exists
My heart will see
Much better than my eyes
The road is light
For a little while
Certainly
I hope
The road will be long
With you.

The Sea Of Fulfillment

I felt your heart
Your breathing
Your heartbeat
Your beautiful bones
Your body stared at me

I touched you
You vibrated silently
Like a leaf in the wind
Like a tuning fork
Before perfect music

I didn't have a hurry
Even though I wanted everything
I proceeded peacefully
Like a cat under the house
I waited
Until the vibration changed to the waves
Suddenly
I was like a ship in the waves
Fulfillment
I also started to vibrate
The resonance
We were one
Me and my sea.

A Simple Paradox And Truth

I'm not a star
Even though I'm made of stars
I'm not the universe
Even though I'm part of the universe
I don't control time
Even though I'm going to measure it

I'm just one atom of time
Together we are
Stars
The universe
Time.

Sum

I look back
There I was

I stand on the line segment
Above the radius
In the curved weather
My cube root
Increasing
On the ice of my life

Time
A strange thing
Sum
I raise a glass.

In Space Love Is Near

I walked a long time
Alone or together
Still alone
Via long straight space roads
Vacuum sounds everywhere

I stopped
At the point where I was
In infinity
I heard better
Myself
And others

You were in it
You had been
You are
Just like you are
I didn't have time to look
Now I see well

Love
Possibility
Me
You
Us
In infinity.

The Strongest Flame

I woke up
To life
I breathe again
Together
We breathe
For love

It's air
Words and bytes
That's the flame
What can't be thought
When is
Internal fire
Me
And your light
A common journey
I love you close
Even though I would be far away.

The Thinking Bodymind

I'm thinking
When I feel the thoughts
I experience
When I feel my life
I feel
When I come true
In my mind

Experience is a compass
Not information or a map
My body pulsates ahead.

The Universe

Emptiness above the sea
And below
Everywhere

Somewhere some sound
An illusion
Existing

Love is a desert
Heart of life
All

Your sea
Your voice
Your life

My life

So are we.

The Universe Is Inside Me

I am here
It's midsummer
The light dazzles me
I think
My life
Myself
I'm happy
All
Small pieces
In the light of my life
Happy from the happiness
To exist
Peace
Is inside me
In my own universe.

My View

I have a view
From there I come
It is worthless
Still it has significance

My view is like a wood
No chair or table
It is not a message
It leaves no sign

My view exists
My view remains.

Where Is The Finder There Is The Seeker

I look at myself in
I focus and I see it
Inside living space
The infinite and universal

I don't have time for a star
I don't need the speed of light
I don't need a telescope
In my view
Everything important

Myself in the universe.

© 2017 Kolamo, Mika
Kustantaja: BoD – Books on Demand, Helsinki, Suomi
Valmistaja: BoD – Books on Demand, Norderstedt, Saksa
ISBN: 978-951-568-284-0